BECOMING

INSTAGRAM

FAMOUS

Removing the Filters and Unearthing the Secrets of
Becoming Famous Online

Ghulam Hassan Yatoo

This Book belongs to

Name : -________________________

Address : -________________________

____

____

 @facebook  @twitter  @instagram

Our book is
related to

*" BECOMING INSTAGRAM FAMOUS " is a Blueprint for
online business owners and entrepreneurs"*

Table of Contents

Chapter 1

Introduction

Most of us dream of becoming famous. Whether if we have talent in acting, singing, writing, dancing, and the list goes on, all of us wanted to be recognized at some point in our life, or we still dream about it until today.

The world is digitalizing, and the internet has made many people's dreams to become famous come true. From Justin Bieber getting discovered on Youtube to Nusr-Et a.k.a Salt Bae whose Instagram video went viral, the list of people getting found on the internet is a long one, and it will not be ending soon.

Today, we live in a world of online celebrities and influencers. There are spectators, and there are those who want to be in the spotlight. Spectators usually are happy to see content from their favorite artists while those who want to be in the spotlight, do everything to get the world's attention.

Social media is oozing with looks and talents. If you are looking for a model, you can find a lot on Instagram. If you need a photographer, you can hire one from Facebook. Do you need a writer? A single tweet can fill your inbox with aspiring writers. The internet and social media have opened a lot of doors to make dreams happen.

A person who has a massive following on social media and is not a celebrity is called an influencer. An influencer usually has a specific genre or theme on their feeds, and a lot of people look up to them. Brands also want to work with them. Being a social media influencer has a lot of perks. Indeed, the new online market allowed people and brands to promote each other with minimal expenses compared to putting your products on a billboard, newspaper, magazine, or even appear on television. Social media influencers make it easier for brands, and even businesses reach a vast audience with just a single post.

A social media influencer can earn in a lot of ways. They can charge for a single photo, video, and even an Instagram story. Rates depend on how big the brand is and how long the business owners expect their products to be showcased by an influencer. For most people, it is easy money. But behind all the glitz, glamour, and pr boxes these influencers receive, are hard work, efforts, and sacrifices. Most of these social media influencers we see online worked their way up to where they are now. Today, many people dream of becoming one of them, but the question is, do they have what it takes?

. In this book, we will not just reveal the secrets of *becoming Instagram famous*. We will also uncover the tricks of the trade on how to become a social media influencer. From learning how to create your own Instagram to learning about engagement rates, engaging with your fans, and sustaining your success, we have got you covered!

In the next six chapters, you will learn how to create your own *Instagram account* and build your following. The process can be hard and long, but we will guide you through it. If you want to become Instagram famous and think you have what it takes, keep reading.

Chapter
2

The Power of Social Media

The world has evolved tremendously. In terms of communication, from letter writing to now connecting to someone by single swipe or click on our phones is possible.

The *advancements made by technology* allow us to connect with our family and friends, but it also allows us to communicate with the world. Today, social media is one of the most powerful tools used to reach our loved ones as well as create a more extensive audience contact if we have a business or if we have talents to share with the world.

Social media stemmed from online messaging platforms like *Yahoo Messenger*. The first social media platforms that we had were MySpace and Friendster. In 2010, social media platforms like Facebook, Twitter, and Instagram took the world by storm. Today, musical apps like *Musical.ly and Tiktok* are popular among internet users.

Social media networking platforms have created a new landscape for *communicating*, *selling*, and even creating new *celebrities*. Aside from allowing you to communicate with *friends and family*, social media provides an avenue to promote your business or your hobbies.

Social Media and Connectivity : *At its core, social media serves as a bridge, connecting people from diverse backgrounds across the globe. The ability tooc communicate instantaneously has revolutionized relationships, making the world feel smaller and more interconnected than ever before.*

Influence on Public Opinion : *Beyond personal connections, social media has become a potent tool in shaping public opinion. From political discourse to cultural trends, platforms like Twitter and Facebook wield significant influence, often molding the narrative in real-time.*

Business and Social Media : *Businesses have not been immune to the allure of social media. In the realm of marketing, savvy companies leverage these platforms to reach their target audience, fostering engagement and building brand loyalty. Notable success stories abound, showcasing the transformative impact of strategic social media campaigns.*

Educational Impact of Social Media *: Education, too, has undergone a digital makeover. Social media platforms offer a treasure trove of educational resources, from online courses to interactive content, revolutionizing the way we learn.*

Challenges and Controversies : *However, the power of social media is not without its challenges. Controversies surrounding misinformation, cyberbullying, and data privacy highlight the need for responsible use and regulation.*

Social Media Trends : *The dynamic nature of social media is reflected in its ever-evolving trends. From the rise of ephemeral content to the integration of augmented reality, staying abreast of these trends is crucial for both users and businesses.*

Innovations in Social Media : *Technological innovations continue to redefine the social media landscape. Features like live streaming, virtual reality, and AI-driven content recommendation algorithms enhance user experience, keeping platforms engaging and relevant.*

The Psychology Behind Social Media : *Delving into the psychology of social media reveals fascinating insights into human behavior. From the addictive nature of scrolling to the influence of online communities, understanding these dynamics is key to navigating the digital realm mindfully.*

Social Media and Activism : *Social media has emerged as a powerful ally in activism. Movements advocating for social change find a global stage, with hashtags and viral campaigns amplifying voices that might otherwise go unheard.*

The power of social media has been strengthened over the years. If you are not yet maximizing your use of social media, here are some benefits you can get from your social media account:

01: *According to the London College of International Business Studies, social media opens you to the opportunity to engage with experts in various fields. Through social media, people who are doing research or have particular fascinations can communicate with the experts in different areas by just leaving a comment or sending these experts a message on their own profiles or pages.*

02: *Another benefit of social media, according to the London College of International Business Studies, is that it enhances learning management systems. It allows schools to can deliver educational programs to their students by utilizing the instant messaging and video functions of social media platforms.*

03: Aside from educational benefits, if you are a budding blogger or video blogger, social networking platforms give you not just access to a bigger audience. Still, it also gives you access to paid advertising services. If you have built a good amount of followers, you can partner with small businesses or brands to start expanding your reach. Some brands will pay you for advertising their products while some will provide you their goods to try giving you more content topics to publish on your page.

04: Joining social networking platforms is free. Of course, to get you started, you need to join social networking platforms. What's good about these platforms is that they provide free sign-up for everyone regardless if it is a personal account or a business account. They will help you make baby steps and even leaps to reach your goals. Social networking platforms also provide you opportunities to reach a wider audience by featuring you or your brand in banners found at social networking sites – this assistance though is not free, and you need to pay a certain amount to activate it.

05: You can be the next online sensation. If you join social networking platforms to pursue your dreams to become a musician, a writer, an actor, or anything you can think of, it provides you your own stage and spotlight to showcase them. A lot of celebrities today have discovered through the internet just by sharing a video or a blog. Managers are also now on the lookout for the next rising star because social media platforms allow them to scan through various talents compared to those they just meet in their offices.

There are still many reasons you should venture out or maximize your social networking platform use. Nevertheless, we also need to tackle some of the cons of using social media to let users know the possible threats to our own health and even security when we use one of them.

01: *When you use social networking platforms, you are opening yourself and some of your private information to everyone. Before the rise of social networking platforms, people led a more private life, and only celebrities reported their lives. Today, social networking platforms encourage you to post anything you want, and sometimes people tend to overshare even the things that could be used against them.*

02: *You can fall victim to identity theft. Identity theft has been around even before social networking platforms. But social networking platforms make it easier for people to commit identity theft since there is more convenient access to photos and information.*

03: *Children are not safe on social networking platforms. The children today are more internet savvy than their parents, and most of the time, they are more prone to false information and predators lurking on the internet. According to psychiatrist, Joseph Austerman, D.O., "with the unchecked use of social media, kids' exposure to misleading and blatantly false information increases exponentially." Aside from the exposure to false information, kids can also be exposed to child predators who will make them believe in lies and ask for money, and in one of the cases in the U.S., inflict self-harm. Kids are also susceptible to cyberbullying if they have social media accounts.*

04: *Hackers can also have easy access to your bank accounts and other private information. Identity theft can also lead to money being withdrawn from your bank account. Some websites that you can go to offer the option of using your social networking site profile to log-in before you make a purchase; this allows them to connect your bank details to your profile. Making sure that you have tight security measurements in your account and also asking your bank to inform you of sketchy transactions are ways to help you protect your hard-earned money.*

Of course, we will not talk about all the social networking platforms and how to turn them into a fan base in the following chapters. In fact, we are only going to talk about how to be Instagram famous, but of course, we want you to be more responsible with your online actions and be more informed with the pros and cons of using social networking platforms.

Knowledge about the internet can be beneficial when you want to expand your reach, and it will help you navigate this digital jungle when you know the pros and cons of the internet.

Chapter 3

Creating Your Own Instagram

Instagram is one of the most popular social networking platforms today. It is a photo and video-sharing platform created by Kevin Systrom and Mike Krieger and is now owned by Facebook Inc.

Instagram is a platform that only allows you to upload photos, and at first, images should fit the 1:1 ratio. Today, Instagram has approved photos and videos to be resized, and more than that, it has provided a new celebrity landscape to its users. Instagram has paved the way for a lot of people to boost their reach. Aspiring models, photographers, artists, and a whole lot more made the platform of their portfolio. Using hashtags in their posts also allows them to be discoverable by people worldwide. Today, Instagram has adopted a new service, which is Instagram Stories, that enables users to share photos and videos that last only up to twenty-four hours. In addition to that, a "highlight" feature is also added so users can keep Instagram stories as highlights. These highlights can be viewed by anyone as long as they are up on the user's profile.

For some people, Instagram may just be another social networking platform, but for brands, celebrities, and influencers, it allows them to generate another market and another source of income. Celebrities like Kim Kardashian and Kendall Jenner would sometimes earn hundreds of thousand dollars just for a product to make its way to their profiles. For some people, that is the dream. But the question is, how do you make it happen?

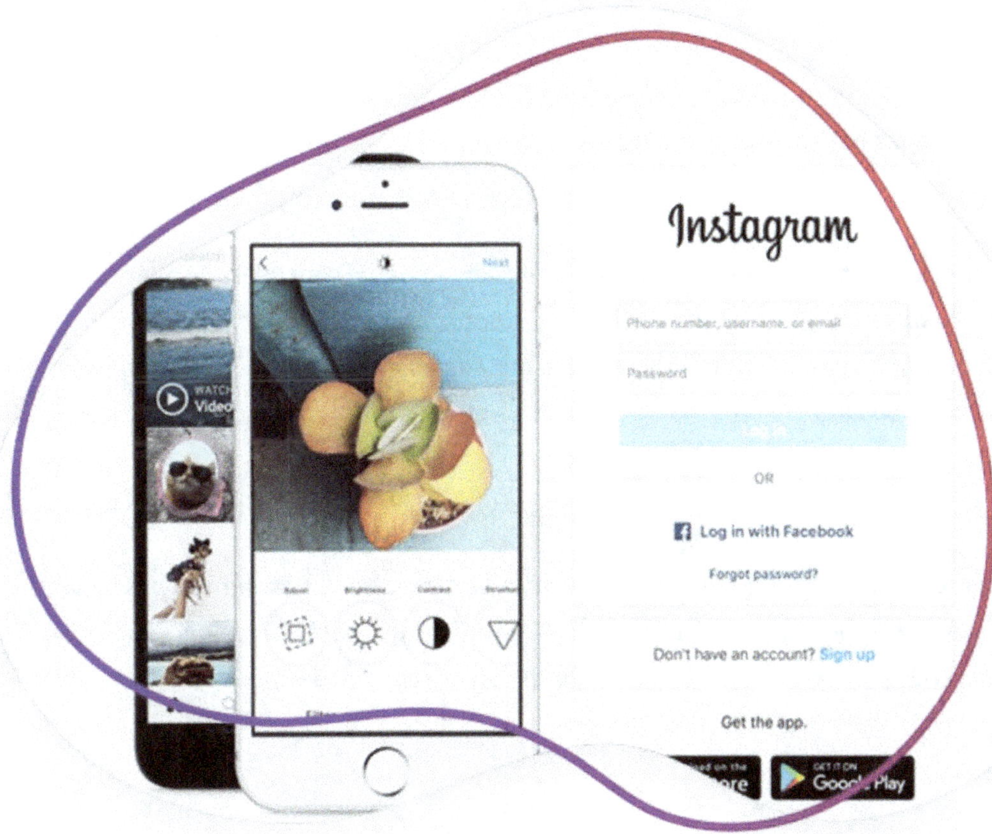

Setting up your own Instagram account is easy. Here are the steps you need to follow according to the Instagram website to get you started:

01: Download the Instagram application from the application store (iPhone) or Google Play Store (Android).

02: Open the application once installed.

03: Tap Sign up with an email or the Phone number (Android) or Create New Account (iPhone), then enter your email address or phone number (which will require a confirmation code) and tap next. You can also tap Log in with Facebook to sign up with your Facebook account.

04: If you register with your email or phone number, create a username and password, fill out your profile info then tap next. If you register with Facebook, you'll be prompted to log into your Facebook account if you are currently logged out.

Here are the steps you need to follow if you want to create an Instagram account from your desktop:

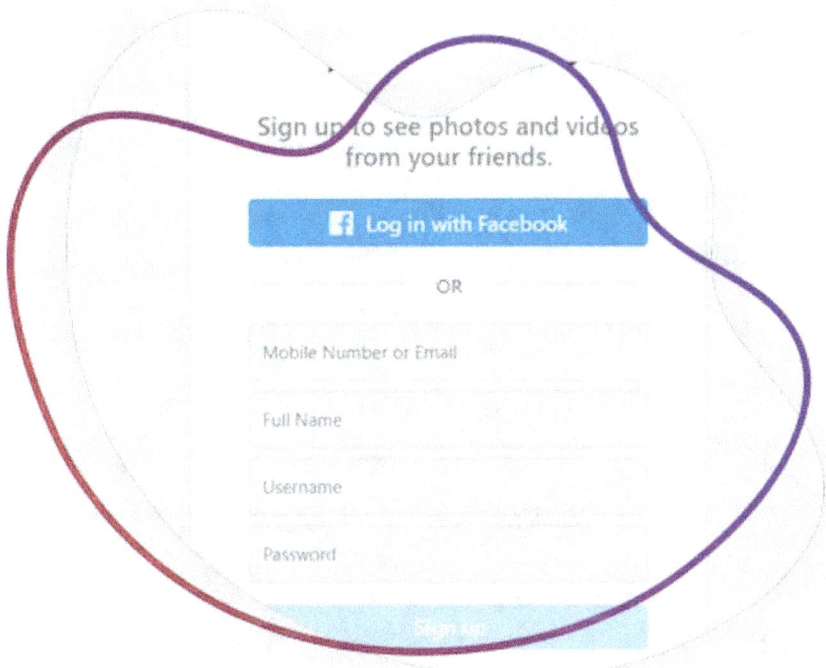

01: Go to Instagram.com

02: Click Sign up, enter your email address, create a username and password, or click Log in with Facebook to sign up with your Facebook account.

03: If you register with an email, click Sign up. If you register with Facebook, you'll be prompted to log into your Facebook account if you're currently logged out.

If you sign up with an email, make sure you enter your email address correctly and choose an email address that only you can access. If you log out and forget your password, you'll need to be able to access your email to get back into your Instagram account.

*Creating your Instagram account is one step towards **becoming Instagram famous.** In the next chapters, we will discuss how you should manage your account from your content plan to engage with your followers.*

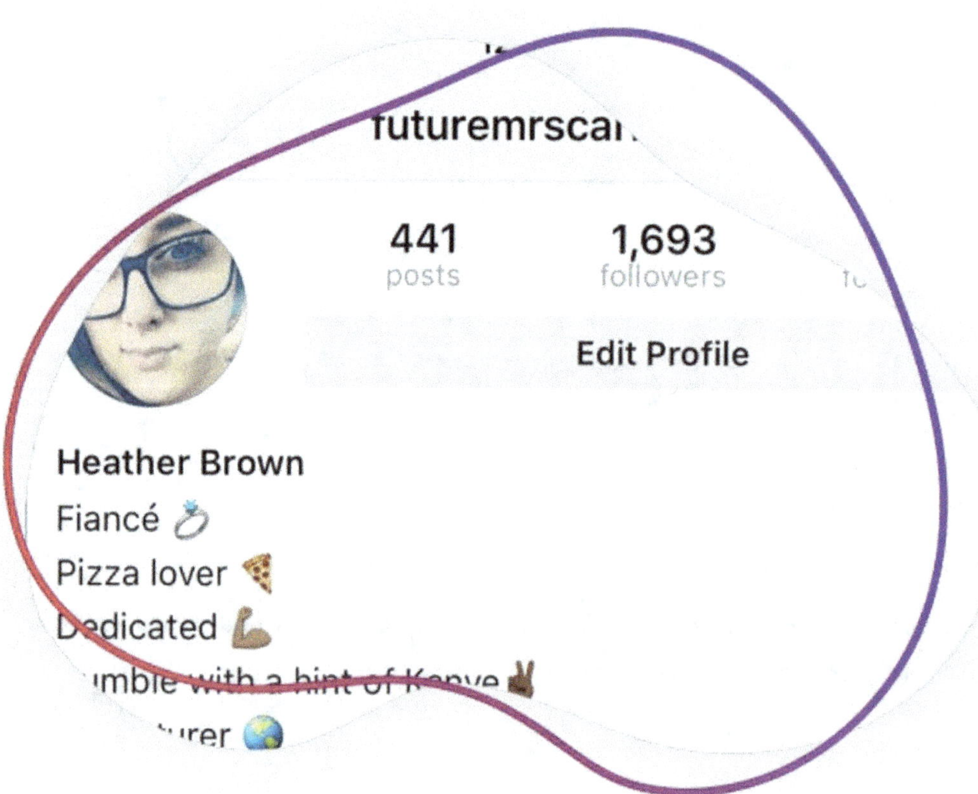

Chapter
4

Creating Your Own Content Plan

"A brand is no longer what we tell the consumer it is – it is what the consumer tells it is." Scott Cook

If you want to **be Instagram famous**, *you need to put a lot of thought in what you want to post. For some people, they really allot a specific time in their day to create content for their accounts. Other people also follow themes to create their Instagram feed more cohesive or appealing to their followers.*

When you want to be Instagram famous, you need to consider more than just your taste or likes. You also need to consider what your followers want to see without compromising your authenticity. **Becoming Instgram famous** *does not happen overnight and it takes time and effort to reach a certain level of popularity before brands and other Instagram celebrities collaborate with you. For now, you need to learn how to make a content plan or a process that will help you build a following or an audience.*

Here are ways on how to create your own content plan and other tips on how to make your Instagram content eye-catching:

The first thing you need to consider in your content plan is to identify what theme you want.

Are you going to publish lifestyle, fashion, music, food, etc.? Knowing what your main subjects will be can help you create a more cohesive feed. Sticking to a theme or more just as long you commit to it will help you brand yourself.

Look for inspiration.

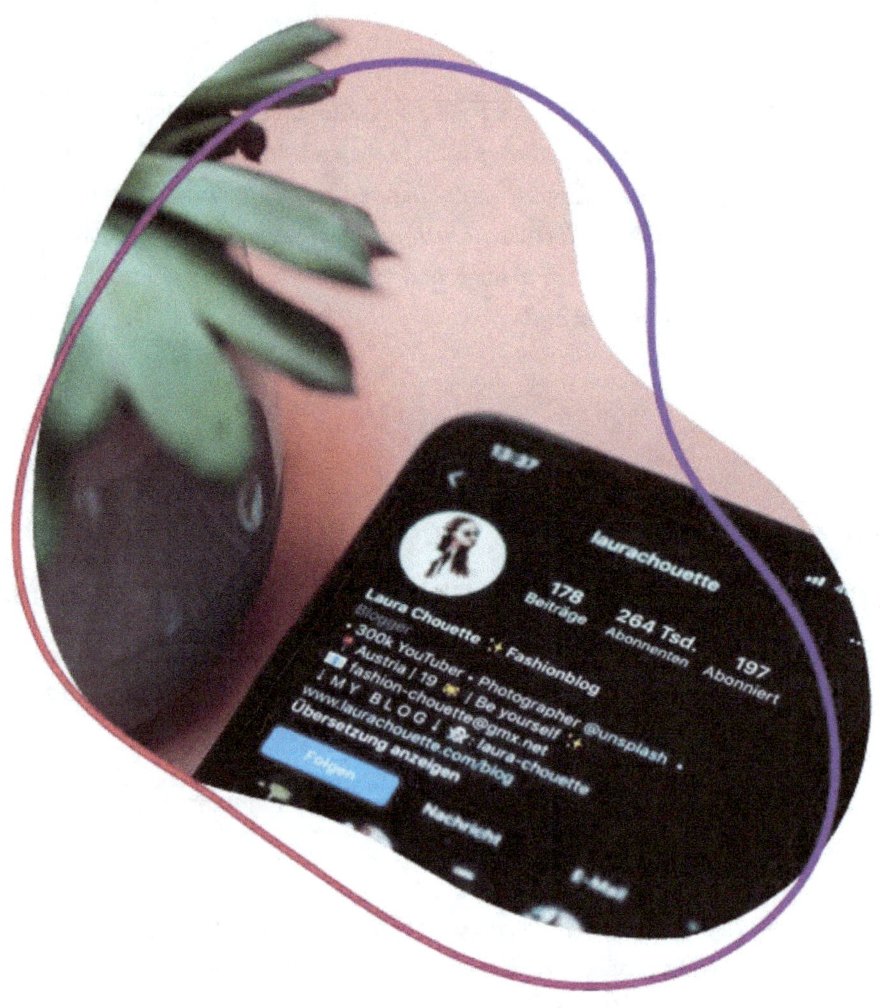

Browsing through profiles that spark your creativity or help you build a vision board is highly recommended. Perhaps, you can also look for styles and source of inspiration from Pinterest. You can also reach out to other Instagram users that you find their contents eye-catching. Remember that the word we're using is "inspiration" and not "imitation".

Source websites or applications that can help improve your content.

There is no secret on how to be Instagram famous. You can all find the answers when you look it up online and one of the secrets or techniques that Instagram-famous people do to make their profiles beautiful is they use applications. Filipina fashion blogger and influencer Camille Co has been constantly sharing the applications she uses and her editing techniques to her followers through her Instagram stories or through her Youtube channel. She reveals the applications she uses as well as a step by step on how she edits her photos and videos to add something extra to a photo.

Make sure you have a schedule of posting.

When you want to be Instagram famous the goal is to be always seen. Planning when and what you post is important. Your followers need to see you even if they are not searching for you. An Instagram algorithm is influenced by the internet, relationships, timeliness, frequency, following and usage. The contents that you and your followers always see on feeds are by those they usually engage with and the more you post, the more you will appear on their recent feed. It may be annoying to some but it can be beneficial to you too.

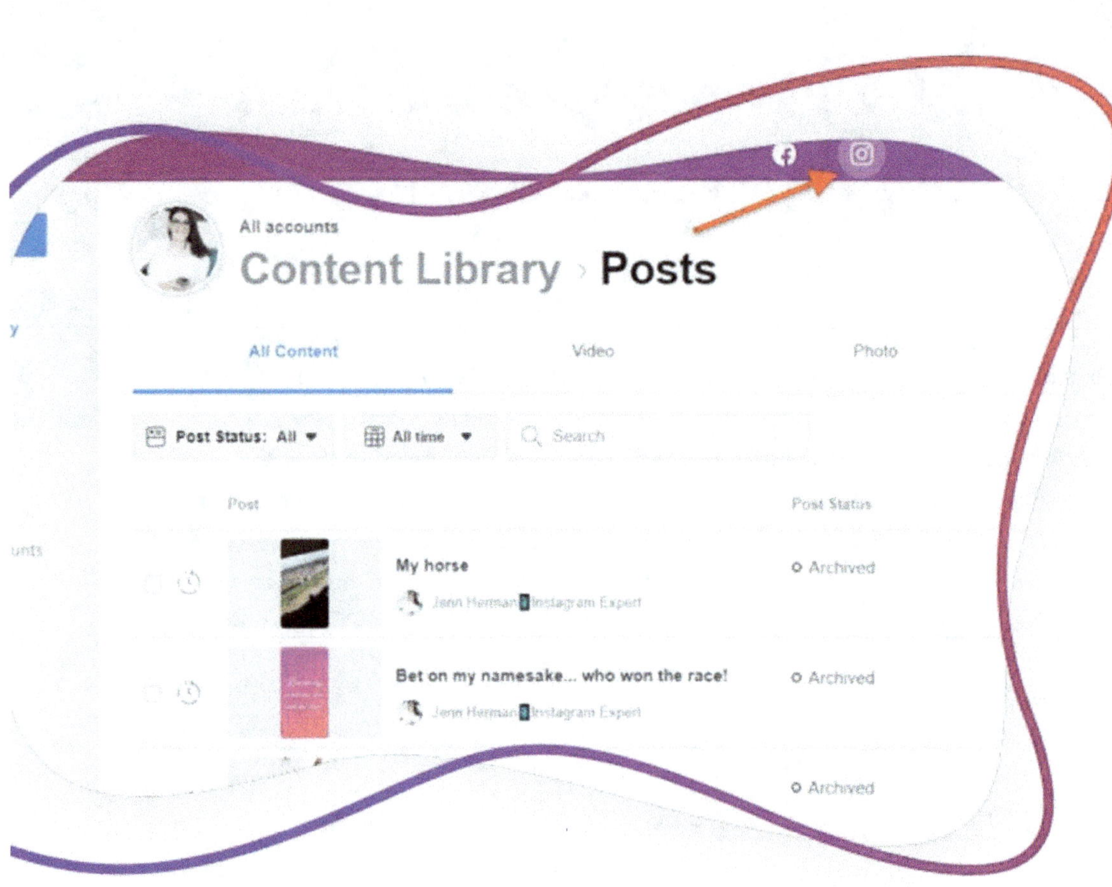

It is also important to identify the chronological order of your posts. How often do you have to insert videos in your feed and how many photos you need up on your profile before uploading a video. Scheduling your posts and identifying which comes first is important to have a diverse content in your profile.

According to social media expert Neil Patel, "If you make a habit of posting several times a day and then transition to only a few times a week, you will start to lose followers and generate less engagement in your post."

Look for the latest trends and learn how to integrate them in your profile.

Nothing catches the eye better than a new trend. Are there viral challenges circulating in the internet? The chances of you reaching a wider audience when you join the bandwagon is high. A lot of people have drawn attention to their profiles by a single photo or video doing an online challenge.

Plan ahead

A content plan is not just about the posts you have to make today and tomorrow. Instagram celebrities and influencers have a long list of soon-to-be posts and maybe that's because they have brand deals or product placements but that should not stop you. It helps when you want to review products, books, or other things that interest you. Posting your reviews does not only give you content but some people might chance upon your post and find it interesting and eventually follow you. It is important that you never run out of content.

There are websites or phone applications that can help you schedule your post such as *Sked*. This application can help you post your content without having to open the application. It also posts your content at the best time of the day where it can get more engagement.

Link your other social media accounts

Growing an online audience is not easy. You need all the help you can get to grow your following and linking your social media accounts and cross-posting your content can get more views than you imagine. When you link your social media accounts together, you are opening your content to cross-posting which allows a larger audience to view your content. Aside from that, not all your Facebook friends are also your Instagram and Twitter followers or vice versa; when they see your post and it is linked to one of your other social media accounts, they will most likely hit that follow button.

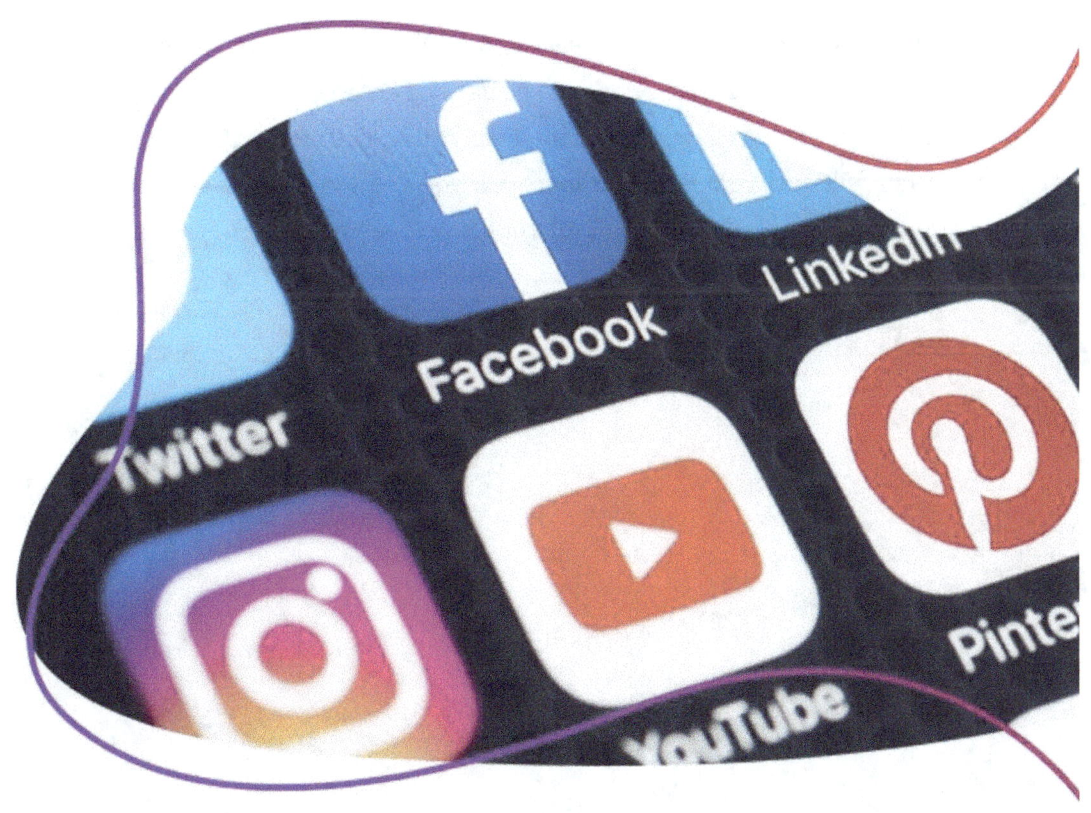

Set your goals

Your goals are an integral part of being Instagram famous. Part of your content plan should be the short-term and long-term goals you want to achieve. By identifying your goals, you have something that will drive you and keep you pushing forward until you reach it.

Your content is the backbone of your goal. It shows who you are and how much you care for your followers. Putting in thought and effort in your content is important because it shows your followers that you are giving an effort to let them know you better.

Making sure that you have a clear content plan to follow gives you a clearer vision on how to achieve your goal. There will be days where there are less engagements with your post but that is okay, do not give up. Even celebrities and social media influencers have their off days. What is important is that you know your goals and every setback, you make sure you have a big comeback.

Chapter
5

Engaging Your Followers

Blogger Sean Gardner once said, "Social media is not just an activity; it is an investment of valuable time and resources. Surround yourself with people who not just support you and stay with you, but inform your thinking about ways to WOW your online presence."

Your followers are the most important aspect in becoming Instagram famous. They become an extension of you in a way that they will also help promote your brand and some even go to the point of defending you fiercely when a rough time comes. All Instagram famous people and even celebrities know that the trust their followers give is vital in their success. Your followers will help you reach your ultimate goal if you treat them right; that is why engaging with them is important.

You should treat your followers like your friends. You do not have divulge all the information of your life to them, but let them feel like you are their friend you can comfortably talk to and vice versa. With that being said, here are ways on how you can engage with your followers:

Like and reply to their comments

One of the simplest ways to show your appreciation to your followers is by liking and replying to their comments on your post. Make a habit of going through the comments section of your post to thank or ask your followers how they are. When you engage with your followers, you are creating a stronger bond with them and they will feel more than a person admiring you from a screen.

Engage them in your Instagram stories

Maximize the use of Instagram by also allowing your followers to engage with you through Instagram stories. Instagram stories allows you to ask questions, make your followers answer polls or trivia questions. Create events they can look forward to like an Instagram question and answer or they can help you choose what you do in a day through polls. Make your followers feel like they are spending the day with you or getting to know you more through Instagram stories.

Chapter
6

Give Back

Another way that you can engage with your followers is by giving back to them. You can host giveaways or schedule meet and greets with them. Showing that you are thankful for their support would mean so much to them especially is most of them look up to you. By giving back to your followers, you are not only showing them of how grateful you are for their support but you are also showing them that they matter and you want to make them happy too.

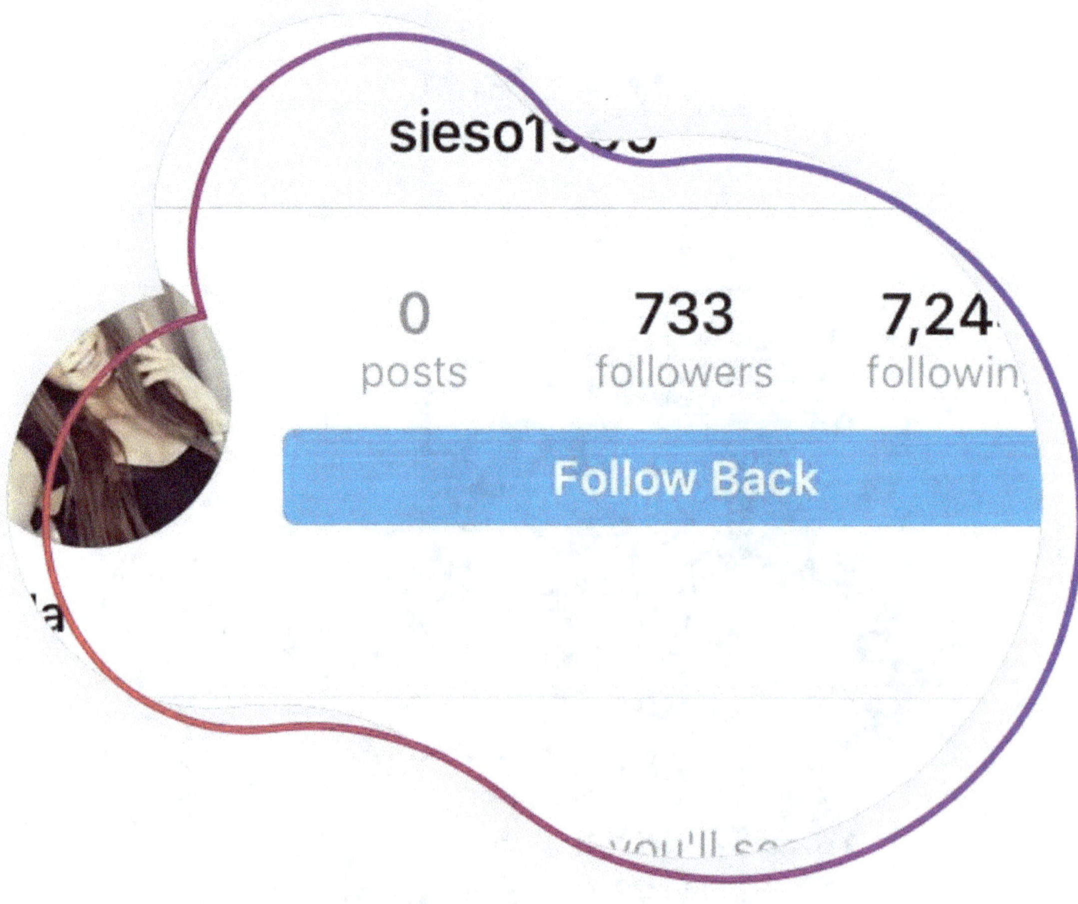

Ask your followers for feedback and content ideas

It is important that your posts are also tailored to your followers likes. Asking them for feedbacks makes them feel heard and part of your circle. When you ask them for feedback, you can know certain areas for improvement and you can come up with content that they will love more. Aside from that, asking your followers for content ideas is smart since you will eventually run out of ideas to make contents of.

Your followers content ideas can range from something creative to something that you will enjoy to something that will make you feel adventurous. Your followers would love to see you do the things they like to do or are yet to experience and is waiting for your review. Always be open to your followers' ideas because they can think of something unique that can help you expand your reach.

Expanding Your Reach

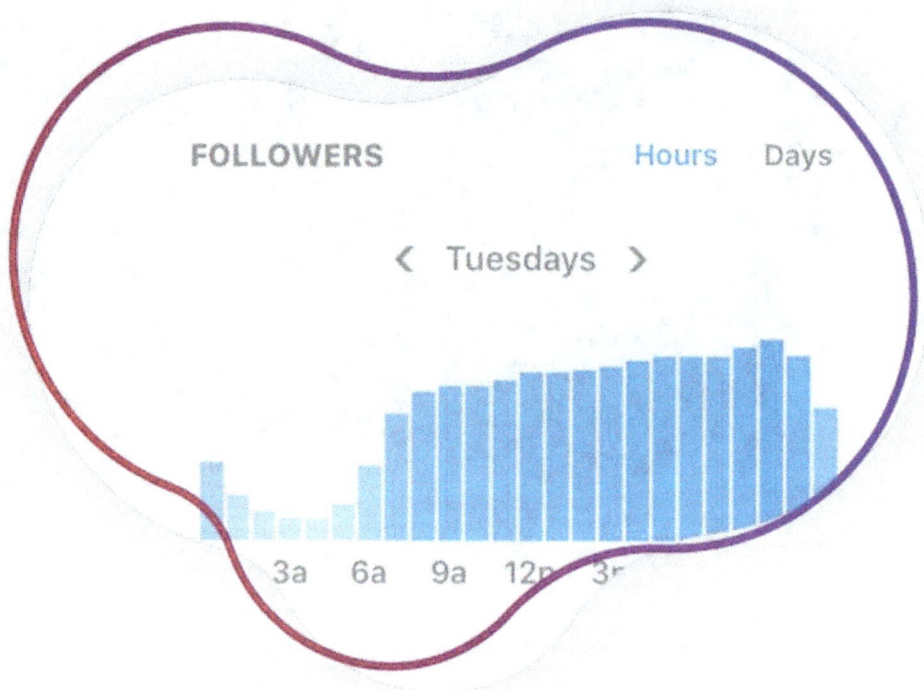

In chapter three, one of the points we made on how to create your own content plan is by linking your other social media accounts to your Instagram. In this chapter, we will discuss why you need to link them and how can you maximize the use of your other social networking platforms as well as tips on increasing your Instagram engagement and what it is for.

Becoming Instagram famous is not just about focusing on Instagram and doing what you can to build your following. If you noticed, celebrities and influencers do not just rely on a single social networking platform to expand their reach. They link their social media accounts and have strategic plans on how and when they publish their contents. Knowing and understanding the science behind boosting your posts' engagement as well as follower count is important. Learning the tricks of the trade will help you expand your reach not just on Instagram but on your other social media accounts as well.

Aside from Instagram, you probably have other social media accounts. Here are the reasons why you should link them:

Businesses have not been immune to the allure of social media. In the realm of marketing, savvy companies leverage these platforms to reach their target audience, fostering engagement and building brand loyalty. Notable success stories abound, showcasing the transformative impact of strategic social media campaigns on Instagram should go on ....

Social media platforms offer a treasure trove of educational resources, from online courses to interactive content, revolutionizing the way we learn.

1. Facebook

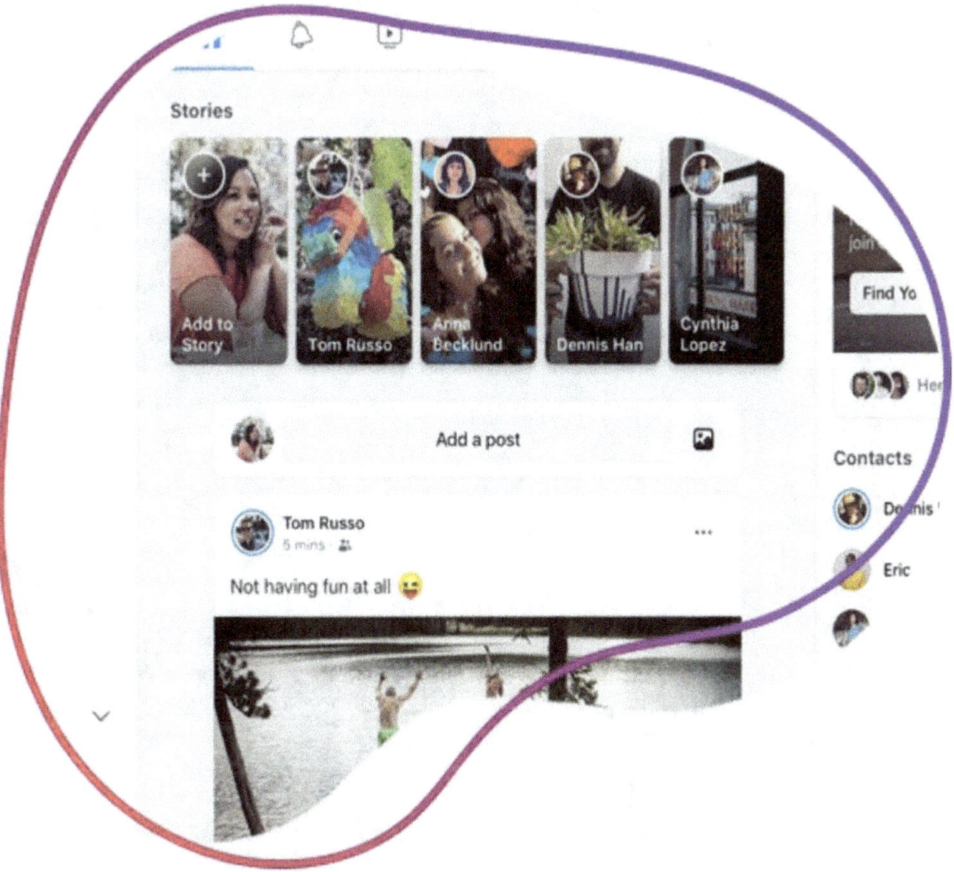

Whether you want to use your personal Facebook or you have a Facebook page, it is easier to build an audience there because of the number of users. You can easily ask your family and friends to share your content and it will gain views or followers instantly. Aside from that, there are also Facebook groups for people who also want to start expanding their social media reach so they create groups to support each other.

1. Facebook

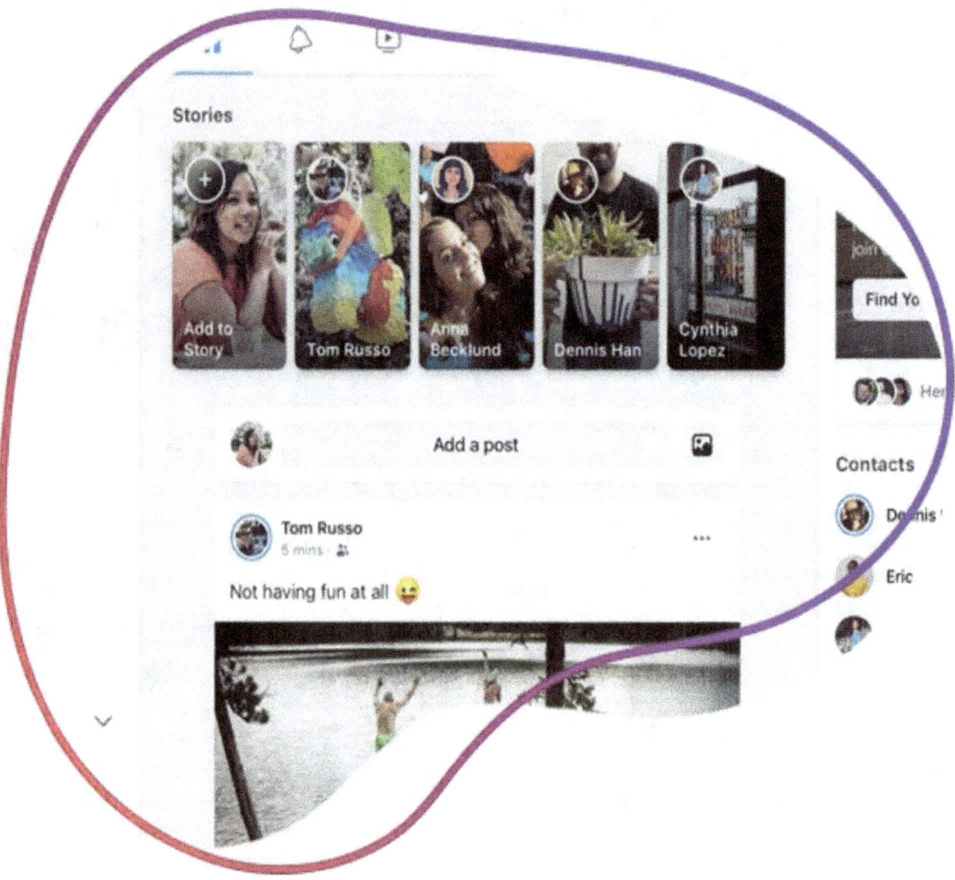

Whether you want to use your personal Facebook or you have a Facebook page, it is easier to build an audience there because of the number of users. You can easily ask your family and friends to share your content and it will gain views or followers instantly. Aside from that, there are also Facebook groups for people who also want to start expanding their social media reach so they create groups to support each other.

2. Twitter

For some people, it's hard to sell brand on Twitter because of the character limit; but that is the challenge. When you master the art of concise and straight to the point captions or descriptions, it will be easier for you to get audience from Twitter. If you are also using a hashtag, there are websites that provide analytics for it and from there, you can analyze your audience information.

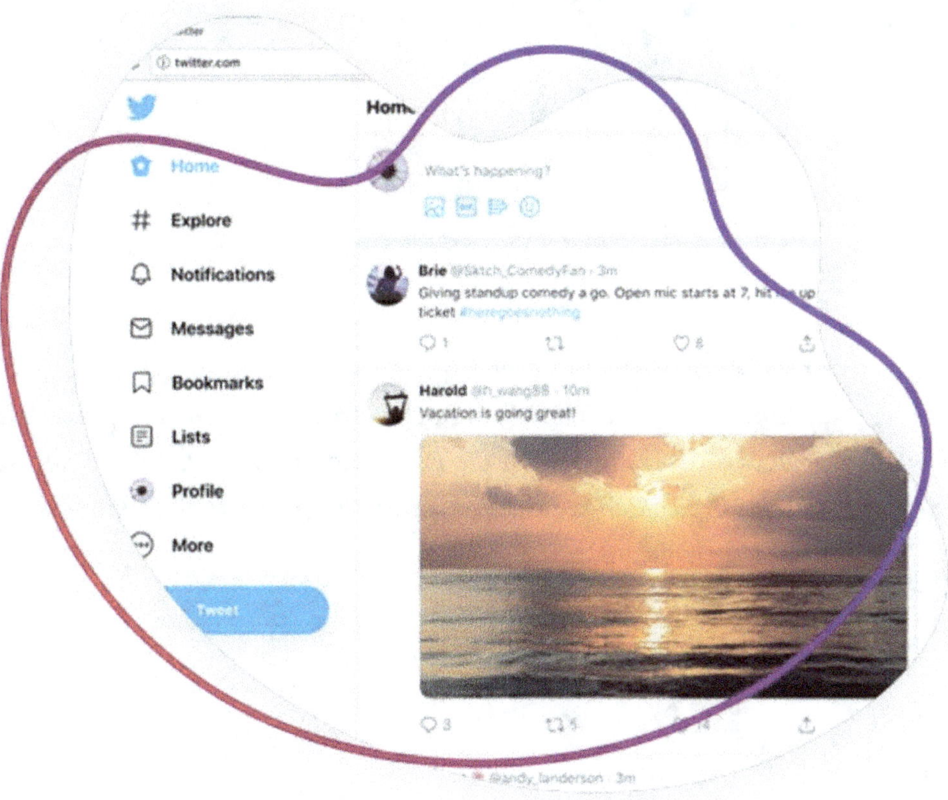

Growing your audience seems easy at first, but when you have a target number of follower goals, the challenge begins. It is important to know the ins and outs of each social media platform to maximize their use in expanding your reach. You can also watch and read tips from people who have successfully grown their follower count and have made it to become Instagram famous.

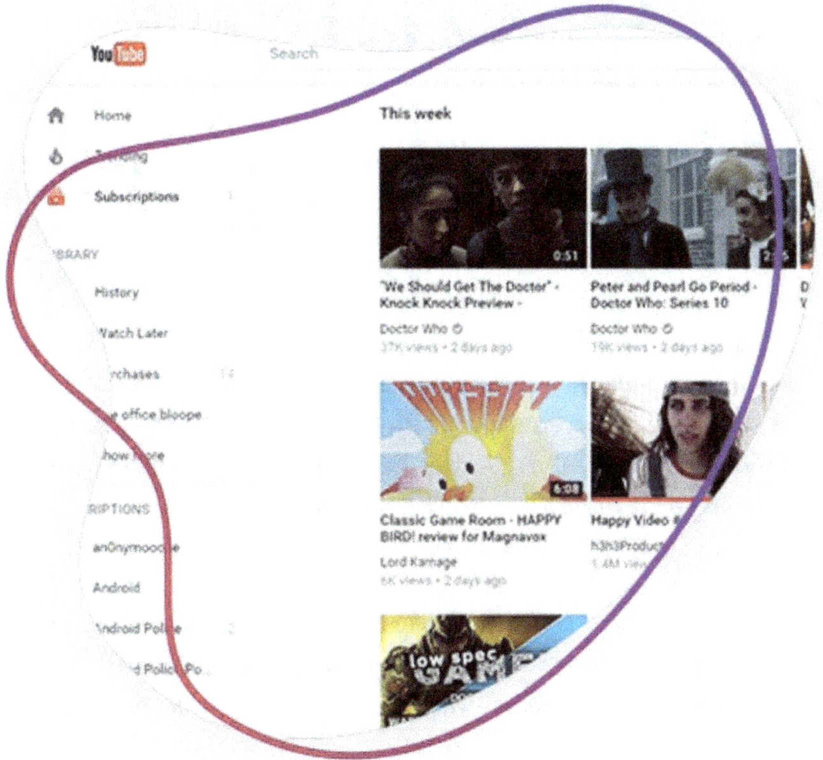

3. Youtube

YouTube is now one of the most popular video streaming social networking platforms. A lot of people like Justin Bieber, Troye Sivan, Madison Beer, and a whole lot more artists were discovered through this platform. Youtube also provides its own analytical system to streamers to help them know what their viewers like and which areas they can improve on. Most youtubers also link their social media accounts in their videos so people who discover their content can check out their other accounts and maybe give it a follow.

4. Other online platforms

Other online platforms are also good avenues to expand your reach. Different online platforms have different algorithms and there are also platforms that have specific discussions. If you have other social networking sites aside from the ones mentioned above, it is best to do research on those so you can understand how to build an audience from there.

Linking your social media accounts together makes it easier for people to discover you. Aside from cross-posting some of your content, you can also release special content per social media site so your followers will make an effort so see it giving you higher engagement in those websites.

When you learn how to manage your social media accounts, the next step you want to do is to measure your engagement rate. Engagement rates matter especially if you have a growing following. Brands who will consider you to collaborate with them looks at your engagement rates to see if you are worth it.

Engagement rates are calculated by the number of people who interact with your profile. Most celebrities have high engagement rates because of their big following. But for some influencers, engagement is key in raising your engagement rates. Here are some of the tips influencers use to increase their engagement rate:

1. *Reply to their followers.*

2. *Ask their followers to comment a word, phrase, emoji, etc. on their recent post if they saw it from their Instagram story.*

3. *Create giveaways that require people to follow them and tag friends.*

4. *Collaborate with other celebrities and influencers and get endorsed by them.*

Growing your audience seems easy at first, but when you have a target number of follower goals, the challenge begins. It is important to know the ins and outs of each social media platform to maximize their use in expanding your reach. You can also watch and read tips from people who have successfully grown their follower count and have made it to become Instagram famous.

Chapter 7

Keeping It Real

> *"Social media will help you build up loyalty of your current customers to the point that they will willingly, and for free, tell others about you."*
> Bonnie Sainsbury

Whether you are reading this book to make yourself an Instagram celebrity or introduce your business to a bigger audience, one of the most important things that you need to always keep in mind when you are venturing out on social media is to keep it real.

Most of the time we hear news about being exposed for who they are not and social media can be a really harsh place when that happens. You will see celebrities and influencers losing followers, businesses having to close down because of boycott, some will even assassinate and spread false information about someone; but that will not happen as long as you keep it real.

You are probably thinking, of course you will keep it real because you want people to know the real you. But in some cases, when people start getting more famous, it does not always keep them good. And sometimes, we think that there are harmless actions we do online but in reality, it is not acceptable to the eyes of others. Here are some ways on how you can keep it real on Instagram:

Get real followers

It is no secret that some celebrities and influencers buy their followers. In December of 2014, Instagram purged fake followers and a lot of celebrities have been exposed for buying fake followers. If you are looking to be Instagram famous, try your best to get real and organic followers. When you start getting a big following and brands are looking to partner with you, they will check your followers and some of them will know if your followers are organic or real.

It is also important that you keep your followers engaged because an account with a big following but with little to no engagement can make people and brands question your authenticity.

Growing your audience seems easy at first, but when you have a target number of follower goals, the challenge begins. It is important to know the ins and outs of each social media platform to maximize their use in expanding your reach. You can also watch and read tips from people who have successfully grown their follower count and have made it to become Instagram famous.

Do not deceive people

Instagram is one of the places where it is easier to manipulate the reality. We see people getting exposed for lying or editing their lifestyle. We have short films dedicated to making people see that behind happy images, there is actually another sad or dangerous life the person lives.

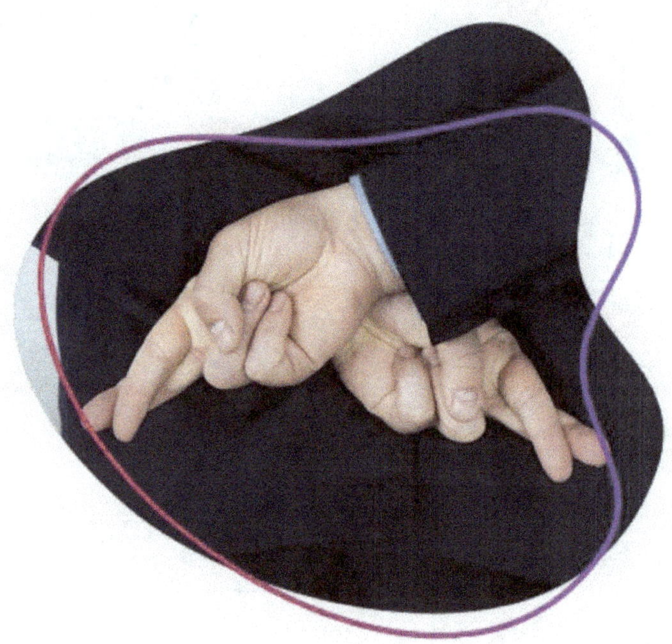

When you want to become Instagram famous, the last thing you want to happen to you is get called out by deceiving people. Always be your true and authentic self even if you are surrounded by more good looking or successful people. People are now getting tired of the perfect life. They are looking for more relatable or more "human" people to follow.

Create your own brand

Nobody likes copycats. People have been trademarking or copyrighting their works left and right. And although someone really fits your vibe, only take inspiration from them but never copy them. While most people look like they are only following for aesthetic purposes, there is still a greater audience who follows someone because they can feel their uniqueness. Make your brand stand out and not blend in, this way, you will be easier to identify and to remember.

Create your own hashtag

When you want to become Instagram famous, you need to set yourself apart from others. Creating a hashtag that is unique to you and your followers will help people identify you more. When you have your own hashtag, people will easily associate the hashtag with you even if your face is not in the content someone posts.

Engage with your followers like you would with your friends

When you treat your followers like how you would treat your friends, it will be easier to strengthen your relationships with them. When you treat your followers how you would treat people in real life, it would be easier for you to make conversation with them. Aside from that, when you show your followers the real you, it will be easier for them to love and understand you.

You can also include your followers' posts as features in your Instagram to show them that you appreciate them.

Talk to people like how you want them to talk to you

Your followers will most likely come from different age groups. Talk to them like how you want to be talked to. People will know a lot about you by how the way you treat others and how you talk to them. Your treat your followers how you treat your friends but always remember that there is a line to draw when it comes to making jokes or talking about sensitive stuff especially online.

Authenticity matters today more than ever. We may be surrounded by more good-looking and more successful people, but it is not a reason to not be yourself. You will reach your goal without having to pretend. Keep on being you and you will attract the right crowd.

Create your own brand

Nobody likes copycats. People have been trademarking or copyrighting their works left and right. And although someone really fits your vibe, only take inspiration from them but never copy them. While most people look like they are only following for aesthetic purposes, there is still a greater audience who follows someone because they can feel their uniqueness. Make your brand stand out and not blend in, this way, you will be easier to identify and to remember.

01: Your content should show a lot of heart and a lot of you.

02: Always find out what your audience wants to see.

03: Never forget to communicate with the people who support you.

04: You should always be inspired to make content that can also inspire thers.

05: It's okay to draw inspiration from others but do not copy them.

06: Always try your best to gain real Instagram followers.

07: Mix up your content once in a while but stay true to your theme.

08: Learn the algorithms of the social media accounts that you have and apply them to how you post and create content.

09: Use Instagram with caution.

10: Becoming Instagram famous is possible.

People who want to be Instagram famous have a reason or two on why they want to make it happen. Anything is possible online just as long as you put it the effort and the time to do it. There will be doubters but let the noise of the people who support you drown them out. If you have something that you want the world to see, now is the time to start and you can do it on Instagram!

Create your own hashtag

When you want to become Instagram famous, you need to set yourself apart from others. Creating a hashtag that is unique to you and your followers will help people identify you more. When you have your own hashtag, people will easily associate the hashtag with you even if your face is not in the content someone posts.

Importance of INSTAGRAM # Hashtags

If given the chance, there are people who would kill to become an online star. Instagram is one of the social media platforms that provides great opportunities to people who have built a huge following. It is also the place where people get a more intimate view of how the rich, beautiful, and successful lives.

Becoming Instagram famous does not happen overnight unless you go viral. But it is not impossible for people who knows the ropes in building their following. When you put on the effort to any goal you want to achieve and you commit to it, no matter how long it takes, you will get there.

When you put this book down and feel you are ready to take on the world of Instagram, always remember these tips and it will surely help you find your success:

Understanding Instagram Algorithm and HashtagsInstagram's algorithm is intricately connected to the usage of hashtags. By incorporating relevant and trending hashtags, users can enhance the visibility of their posts, ensuring they reach a broader audience.

Popular and Trending Hashtags : The world of hashtags is dynamic, with popularity and trends constantly evolving. Researching and utilizing popular and trending hashtags in different niches can catapult a post into the spotlight, exposing it to a vast and diverse audience.

Branding with Hashtags : Branded hashtags play a pivotal role in establishing and promoting brand identity. Creating unique, memorable hashtags not only contributes to brand recognition but also fosters a sense of community among followers.

Community Building Through Hashtags : Hashtags serve as virtual meeting points for users with common interests. Successful community-building campaigns often revolve around specific hashtags that unite individuals, creating a shared space for engagement.

Increasing Post Reach with Hashtags : Choosing the right mix of hashtags is an art. Striking a balance between niche-specific and broad hashtags ensures that posts reach the maximum audience while maintaining relevance to the content.

Event Promotion and Hashtags :Events, both online and offline, benefit immensely from event-specific hashtags. These hashtags not only promote the event but also encourage attendee engagement, transforming the event experience into a shared narrative.

. Instagram Stories and Hashtags : Instagram Stories provide a unique opportunity to integrate hashtags seamlessly. Strategic use of hashtags in Stories enhances discoverability and engagement, creating a more immersive experience for followers.

.

Hashtags in Influencer Marketing: In the realm of influencer marketing, hashtags play a crucial role in amplifying campaign reach. Collaborating with influencers who skillfully incorporate relevant hashtags can significantly impact the success of a campaign.

Analyzing Hashtag Performance: Understanding the performance of hashtags is key to refining strategies. Utilizing analytics tools to track hashtag performance allows users to adapt their approach based on real-time data.

Optimizing Hashtags for SEO: The relationship between hashtags and search engine optimization (SEO) should not be underestimated. Strategic hashtag usage can extend the discoverability of content beyond the confines of Instagram, reaching audiences through search engines.

Hashtags Dos and Don'ts: Effective hashtag usage comes with a set of best practices. Simultaneously, avoiding common mistakes such as overloading posts with irrelevant hashtags ensures that the chosen hashtags contribute positively to post visibility.

Industry-Specific Hashtags: Tailoring hashtags to the industry is crucial for establishing relevance and authority. Industry-specific hashtags connect content with like-minded individuals, fostering engagement within niche communities.

Encouraging User-Generated Content with Hashtags: Brands can leverage hashtags to encourage followers to generate content. User-generated content not only serves as authentic endorsements but also strengthens the bond between the brand and its community.

Conclusion

In conclusion, Instagram hashtags are not mere symbols; they are dynamic tools that can elevate content, enhance engagement, and contribute to brand identity. Embracing the multifaceted role of hashtags unlocks the potential for improved visibility and meaningful connections on the platform.

The Power of
Social Media Marketing

The world has evolved tremendously. In terms of communication, from letter writing to now connecting to someone by single swipe or click on our phones is possible. Learn and Expore the new things....

Some important FAQ'S

1. How many hashtags should I use in a single Instagram post?

   The optimal number of hashtags varies, but using a mix of niche-specific and popular hashtags (around 10-15) is a good starting point.

2. Can I use the same hashtags for every post?

   While consistency is essential, it's advisable to tailor your hashtags to each post's content to maximize relevance.

3. Do hashtags work the same way in Instagram Stories?

   Yes, hashtags in Instagram Stories can improve discoverability and engagement, similar to regular posts.

4. How can I track the performance of my hashtags?

   Utilize Instagram Insights or third-party analytics tools to monitor the reach and engagement of your hashtags.

5. Should I create my own branded hashtags?

Absolutely! Branded hashtags contribute to brand identity and community building, fostering a unique space for your audience.

Today, we live in a world of online celebrities and influencers. There are spectators, and there are those who want to be in the spotlight. Spectators usually are happy to see content from their favorite artists while those who want to be in the spotlight, do everything to get the world's attention. Make possible. to achieve

the successful internet marketing goals....

THANKS!

Thank You

We Welcome Your Feedback.

Feel free to get in touch with us for any
feedback or question and comment on central page.